MONEY LIKE MAGIC

Unlocking the Secrets of Wealth Creation

By Louis Sefer

Copyright © 2023

Terms and Conditions
LEGAL NOTICE

Table of Contents

Preface

"Money Like Magic" is more than just a book; it's a blueprint to unlocking the unlimited potential of your mind and manifesting the wealth and abundance you desire. This book is for anyone who has ever felt trapped in a cycle of financial struggle and is ready to break free.

You'll learn how to harness the power of manifestation and tap into the universe's boundless resources to achieve your financial goals. You'll discover the connection between your thoughts and beliefs and your ability to manifest wealth and learn how to shift limiting beliefs that have been holding you back.

Through visualization techniques, affirmations, and journaling exercises, you'll learn how to manifest wealth and abundance in your life. You'll also be introduced to real-life success stories and case studies that demonstrate the power of manifestation, and gain insights and lessons that can be applied to your own journey.

This book will empower you to take control of your financial future and manifest the life of your dreams. It's a call to action, to take the reins of your life, and to change the course of your financial destiny. So, let's begin the journey to manifesting wealth and abundance together.

Introduction

Welcome to the world of manifestation, where the power of your thoughts and beliefs can unlock the doors to unlimited wealth and abundance. This is the first step on a journey to unlock the true potential of your mind and tap into the boundless resources of the universe.

In this introduction, we will explore the power of manifestation, the connection between your thoughts and beliefs and your ability to manifest wealth, and the purpose of this book. We will delve into the world of manifestation and understand the mechanics of how it works, and how you can use it to achieve your financial goals.

You may be wondering how it's possible to manifest wealth, but the truth is that it has been done by countless individuals throughout history. From ancient philosophers to modern-day entrepreneurs, people have been harnessing the power of manifestation to achieve their financial goals for centuries.

Imagine being able to manifest the life of your dreams, without being held back by limiting beliefs or financial struggles. Imagine being able to achieve financial freedom and live the life you've always wanted. This is what this book is all about, empowering you to take control of your financial future and manifest the wealth and abundance you desire.

Are you ready to change the course of your financial destiny? Are you ready to unlock the true potential of your mind and tap into the boundless resources of the universe? Then let's dive into the world of manifestation and begin the journey to manifesting wealth and abundance together.

The Power of Manifestation

The power of manifestation has been long understood by ancient philosophers and spiritual leaders, but it is only in recent times that the scientific community has begun to understand and explore its potential. Manifestation is the process of bringing something into reality through the power of thought and belief. It is the ability to align your thoughts, emotions, and actions with your desired outcome, and bring it into being.

The power of manifestation is not just limited to financial wealth and abundance, it can be applied to any area of your life. From health and wellness, to relationships, to career and personal growth, the power of manifestation can be used to manifest anything you desire.

But what sets manifestation apart from simple wishful thinking or positive affirmations, is that it requires a deep understanding of the connection between your thoughts, emotions, and actions, and the power of aligning them with your desired outcome. It requires a shift in mindset and a change in perspective, from a lack-based mindset to one of abundance and possibility.

Imagine being able to manifest the life of your dreams, by aligning your thoughts, emotions and actions with the things you desire. Imagine being able to manifest wealth,

abundance, and financial freedom, by
understanding the power of manifestation and
harnessing it to your advantage. This is what
this book is all about, empowering you to
understand the power of manifestation and use
it to achieve your financial goals and live the
life you've always wanted.

The Connection Between Thoughts and Wealth

The connection between our thoughts and
our ability to manifest wealth is a fundamental
principle of manifestation. Our thoughts,
beliefs, and emotions shape our reality, and
they play a critical role in our ability to
manifest wealth and abundance.

The idea that our thoughts can shape our
reality is not new, ancient philosophers and
spiritual leaders have understood this
connection for centuries. But modern science
has begun to understand the power of our
thoughts and how they can influence our
reality. Studies have shown that our thoughts
can affect our biology, our behavior, and even
the way we perceive the world around us.

The connection between thoughts and
wealth is a two-way street. On one hand, our
thoughts and beliefs can limit our ability to
manifest wealth, by creating a lack-based
mindset that sees financial struggles as
inevitable. On the other hand, our thoughts
and beliefs can also empower us to manifest
wealth, by shifting our mindset to one of
abundance and possibility.

Think about it, our thoughts shape our reality, and if we believe that we are not capable of achieving financial success, or that wealth is not for us, it will become a self-fulfilling prophecy. But if we change our thoughts and beliefs to align with financial success and abundance, we open ourselves up to the possibility of manifesting wealth.

The power of our thoughts is undeniable, and it is the key to unlocking the unlimited potential of our mind and manifesting the wealth and abundance we desire. This book is about understanding the connection between thoughts and wealth and harnessing the power of our thoughts to manifest the financial success and abundance we desire.

The Purpose of the Book

The purpose of this book is to empower you to take control of your financial future and manifest the wealth and abundance you desire. It's a guide to understanding the power of manifestation and how to harness it to achieve your financial goals. It's a call to action, to take the reins of your life and change the course of your financial destiny.

This book will help you to understand the connection between your thoughts, beliefs, and actions, and your ability to manifest wealth. You'll learn how to shift limiting beliefs and mindsets that have been holding you back, and how to align your thoughts, emotions, and actions with your desired outcome.

You will also learn techniques for manifesting wealth, such as visualization, affirmations, and journaling, and you will be introduced to real-life success stories and case studies that demonstrate the power of manifestation.

The purpose of this book is not just to provide you with information, but to empower you to take action and manifest the life of your dreams. It's about understanding the power of manifestation and using it to achieve financial success and live the life you've always wanted.

Are you ready to take control of your financial future? Are you ready to manifest the wealth and abundance you desire? Then let's dive into the world of manifestation and begin the journey to financial success and abundance together.

Understanding Your Beliefs

The first step in manifesting wealth and abundance is understanding your beliefs about money and wealth. Our beliefs shape our reality and they play a critical role in our ability to manifest wealth.

In this chapter, we will explore the beliefs that shape your relationship with money and wealth. You will learn how to identify limiting beliefs that have been holding you back and how to shift them to align with abundance and financial success.

One of the most common limiting beliefs is the belief that there is not enough money to go around. This belief creates a scarcity mindset that sees financial struggles as inevitable. Another limiting belief is the belief that wealthy people are greedy or that money is evil. These beliefs create a resistance to wealth and abundance and make it difficult to manifest financial success.

You will also learn about the power of positive affirmations and how they can be used to shift limiting beliefs and align your thoughts with abundance and financial success.

This chapter will also cover the importance of understanding your relationship with money and how it has been shaped by your childhood experiences, cultural influences, and societal expectations. By understanding your beliefs about money, you will be better equipped to shift them and align them with abundance and financial success.

Are you ready to understand your beliefs about money and wealth? Are you ready to shift limiting beliefs and align your thoughts with abundance and financial success? Then let's dive into understanding your beliefs and manifesting the wealth and abundance you desire.

Identifying Limiting Beliefs

One of the most important steps in manifesting wealth and abundance is identifying the limiting beliefs that have been holding you back. Limiting beliefs are negative thoughts or convictions that limit your ability to manifest wealth and abundance.

To identify limiting beliefs, it's helpful to pay attention to the thoughts that come up when you think about money or wealth. For example, if you find yourself thinking "I'll never be able to afford that" or "Money doesn't grow on trees", these are signs of limiting beliefs.

Another way to identify limiting beliefs is to look at the areas of your life where you're struggling financially. For example, if you're constantly living paycheck to paycheck, it's a sign that you have a limiting belief about money and abundance.

It's also helpful to pay attention to your feelings when you think about money and wealth. If you feel anxious, stressed or overwhelmed, it's a sign that you have limiting beliefs about money and abundance.

Once you've identified your limiting beliefs, you can start to shift them and align them with abundance and financial success. This can be done by using positive affirmations, visualization, and other manifestation techniques.

It's important to keep in mind that limiting beliefs can be deeply ingrained and shifting them can take time and consistent effort. But with the right tools and techniques, you can align your thoughts, emotions and actions with abundance and financial success, and manifest the wealth and abundance you desire.

The Role of Mindset in Manifestation

The role of mindset in manifestation cannot be overstated, as it plays a critical role in shaping our reality and our ability to manifest wealth and abundance. Our mindset is the collection of thoughts, beliefs, and attitudes that we hold about ourselves and the world around us, and it shapes the way we see and interact with the world.

A mindset of scarcity, for example, sees financial struggles as inevitable, and makes it difficult to manifest wealth and abundance. On the other hand, a mindset of abundance sees financial success as possible and opens up the possibility of manifesting wealth and abundance.

It's important to understand that our mindset is not fixed, it's malleable, and with the right tools and techniques, we can change our mindset to align with abundance and financial success. One of the most effective ways to change our mindset is by using positive affirmations, visualization, and other manifestation techniques.

It's also important to surround ourselves with positive influences and to actively seek out information and experiences that support a mindset of abundance. This can include reading books and articles about manifestation and wealth, listening to podcasts or attending workshops and seminars on the topic.

In order to manifest wealth and abundance, we must first change our mindset to align with abundance and financial success. It's not always easy, but with consistent effort, it is possible to change our mindset and manifest the life of our dreams.

Shifting Your Beliefs to Attract Wealth

Shifting your beliefs is a crucial step in manifesting wealth and abundance. Our beliefs shape our reality, and by shifting limiting beliefs, we can align ourselves with abundance and financial success.

To shift limiting beliefs, it's essential to understand the nature of beliefs. Beliefs are not facts, they are thoughts and perceptions that we hold to be true. And, while they may have been formed based on past experiences and information, they don't necessarily reflect present reality.

One effective way to shift limiting beliefs is to challenge them with evidence and replace them with empowering beliefs. For example, if you believe "Money is hard to come by" or "I'm not good with money", you can challenge these beliefs by finding examples of people who have abundance and financial success and remind yourself that you too can have that success.

Another effective way to shift limiting beliefs is to use visualization and affirmations. Visualization involves creating a mental image of yourself achieving your financial goals, while affirmations are positive statements that you repeat to yourself to change your mindset and align it with abundance and financial success.

It's also important to surround yourself with supportive people and environments that align with your new beliefs. This can include reading books and articles, listening to podcasts, attending workshops and seminars, and even seeking out mentors and role models who embody the beliefs and financial success you desire.

Shifting your beliefs takes time and effort, but it's a vital step in manifesting wealth and abundance. By aligning your thoughts, emotions, and actions with abundance and financial success, you will open yourself up to manifesting the life of your dreams.

Are you ready to shift your beliefs and align them with abundance and financial success? Are you ready to manifest the wealth and abundance you desire? Then let's dive into understanding the process of shifting your beliefs and begin the journey to financial success and abundance together.

Setting and Achieving Financial Goals

Setting and achieving financial goals is an essential step in manifesting wealth and abundance. It's important to have a clear and specific idea of what you want to achieve financially, and to create a plan to make it a reality.

In this chapter, we will cover the steps involved in setting and achieving financial goals. We will begin by discussing the importance of setting SMART goals, which are Specific, Measurable, Achievable, Relevant, and Time-bound.

Next, we will cover the importance of creating a budget and tracking your expenses. This will help you to understand where your money is going and to make adjustments to your spending as needed to achieve your financial goals.

We will also discuss the importance of creating multiple streams of income and diversifying your investments. This can include starting a side business, investing in stocks or real estate, or starting a passive income stream.

Additionally, this chapter will cover the importance of developing the right mindset and habits for achieving financial success. This can include things like learning to delay gratification, practicing gratitude, and developing the discipline to save and invest.

Finally, we will discuss the importance of taking action and staying committed to your financial goals. Achieving financial success requires consistent effort and the determination to see your plan through to completion.

Are you ready to set and achieve your financial goals? Are you ready to manifest the wealth and abundance you desire? Then let's dive into understanding the process of setting and achieving financial goals and begin the journey to financial success and abundance together.

Defining Your Financial Vision

Defining your financial vision is an essential step in manifesting wealth and abundance. It's important to have a clear and specific idea of what you want to achieve financially, and to create a plan to make it a reality. But before you can set specific and measurable financial goals, you need to have a clear understanding of what your financial vision is.

Your financial vision should be more than just numbers, it should be a holistic picture of the life you want to create for yourself and your loved ones. It should encompass not just your financial goals, but also your values, your passions, and your aspirations.

Start by asking yourself questions like: What do I want to achieve financially? How do I want to live? What kind of lifestyle do I want to have? What are my values and how do they relate to my financial vision?

Take the time to really visualize and imagine the life you want to live. Create a detailed and vivid mental picture of your ideal life, and let that guide you in setting your financial goals.

It's also important to remember that your financial vision is not set in stone, it can and should evolve over time. As you achieve certain financial goals and milestones, your vision may change and you should adjust your financial plan accordingly.

Keep in mind that having a clear financial vision is not only important to motivate and guide you, but it also will help you to stay focused and persistent when faced with obstacles and setbacks on your journey to financial success.

Creating a Plan to Achieve Your Goals

Once you have a clear and specific financial vision, the next step is to create a plan to achieve your goals. This plan should include specific and measurable goals, as well as a timeline for achieving them.

Start by breaking down your financial vision into smaller, more manageable goals. For example, if your financial vision includes buying a house, your first goal might be to save a certain amount of money for a down payment.

Next, create a timeline for achieving each goal. This will help you stay on track and motivated as you work towards your financial vision. It's also important to include milestones along the way to help you measure progress and stay motivated.

In addition to setting specific goals, it's important to have a plan for achieving them. This might include creating a budget, cutting expenses, increasing income, or investing in assets.

It's also important to have a plan for overcoming obstacles and setbacks. This might include creating an emergency fund, having a plan for reducing debt, or having a support system in place to help you stay on track.

Creating a plan to achieve your financial goals requires discipline, focus, and commitment. It's important to review your plan regularly and make adjustments as needed.

Overcoming Obstacles and Staying Motivated

Achieving financial success is not always a linear process, and it's important to be prepared for obstacles and setbacks. It's also important to have strategies in place to stay motivated and on track towards your financial goals.

One of the most important things is to have a support system in place. This can include friends and family who believe in your goals and are willing to support you, as well as a financial mentor or coach who can provide guidance and accountability.

Another important strategy is to stay flexible and be willing to adjust your plan as needed. Sometimes things don't go as expected and you may need to re-evaluate your goals and make adjustments to your plan.

It's also important to have a plan for dealing with unexpected expenses or emergencies. This might include having an emergency fund in place or having a strategy for reducing debt.

It's also important to have a plan for staying motivated. This might include setting small rewards for reaching milestones, reminding yourself of the reasons why you set your financial goals in the first place, or finding inspiration from others who have achieved financial success.

Finally, it's important to remember that setbacks and obstacles are a normal part of the process. It's important to be patient and persistent in working towards your financial goals.

Techniques for Manifesting Wealth

Manifesting wealth and abundance requires more than just setting financial goals and creating a plan to achieve them. It also requires developing the right mindset and habits and utilizing specific techniques to attract wealth and abundance into your life.

In this chapter, we will cover some of the most powerful techniques for manifesting wealth.

A. The Law of Attraction: The Law of Attraction states that we can attract into our lives whatever we focus on. To manifest wealth and abundance, it's important to focus your thoughts and energy on prosperity and abundance, rather than lack and scarcity. This can be done through visualization, affirmations, and gratitude practices.

B. Mindfulness and Gratitude: Being mindful and practicing gratitude can help you to cultivate a positive mindset and attract abundance into your life. By focusing on the present moment and expressing gratitude for what you have, you can shift your focus from lack and scarcity to abundance and prosperity.

C. Affirmations: Affirmations are powerful tools for reprogramming your subconscious mind and manifesting wealth. Repeat positive affirmations related to wealth and abundance on a daily basis, it will help to change your mindset and attract wealth and abundance into your life.

D. Visualization: Visualization is a powerful technique for manifesting wealth and abundance. By visualizing yourself in a prosperous and abundant state, you can attract that energy and manifestation into your life.

E. Action: Ultimately, manifesting wealth and abundance requires taking action. It's important to be proactive in working towards your financial goals and to be persistent in the face of obstacles and setbacks.

By utilizing these techniques and developing the right mindset and habits, you can manifest the wealth and abundance you desire. Are you ready to manifest wealth and abundance in your life? Then let's dive into understanding these techniques and continue the journey to financial success and abundance together.

Visualization Techniques

Visualization is a powerful technique for manifesting wealth and abundance. By visualizing yourself in a prosperous and abundant state, you can attract that energy and manifestation into your life.

Here are some visualization techniques that can help you manifest wealth and abundance:

1. Mind Movie: Create a short video that includes pictures, videos and affirmations of your financial goals and the lifestyle you want to create. Watch it regularly to keep your focus on your goals.

2. Mental Rehearsal: Close your eyes and imagine yourself achieving your financial goals. See yourself in vivid detail, living the life you want and having the wealth and abundance you desire.

3. Vision Board: Create a vision board that includes pictures, words, and symbols that represent your financial goals and the life you want to create. Review it regularly to keep your focus on your goals.

4. Guided visualization: Listen to guided visualization audio that leads you through a visualization of achieving your financial goals.

5. Reality Testing: Imagine yourself already having achieved your financial goals, and then think about how it would feel, what you would do, and how your life would change.

Visualization is not just a form of daydreaming, it's a powerful tool for manifestation and it can help you to change your mindset and attract wealth and abundance into your life. By using the visualization techniques regularly, you will be able to focus your mind on what you want and to create a positive and productive mindset that will help you to achieve your financial goals.

Affirmations and Positive Thinking

Affirmations and positive thinking are powerful tools for reprogramming your subconscious mind and manifesting wealth. They can help you to change your mindset and attract wealth and abundance into your life.

Here are some ways to use affirmations and positive thinking to manifest wealth and abundance:

1. Affirmations: Repeat positive affirmations related to wealth and abundance on a daily basis. Some examples of affirmations include "I am rich and successful", "Money flows easily and abundantly into my life", "I am worthy of financial abundance".

2. Positive Thinking: Practice positive thinking by focusing on the good things in your life, and by looking for the positive in every situation. This will help you to cultivate a positive mindset and attract abundance into your life.

3. Gratitude: Practice gratitude by expressing appreciation for the good things in your life, and by focusing on what you have rather than what you lack. This will help you to shift your focus from lack and scarcity to abundance and prosperity.

4. Mindset Shift: Be aware of your thoughts and beliefs about money and wealth. Identify any limiting beliefs and replace them with positive and empowering ones.

5. Mindful Breathing: Incorporate mindful breathing techniques before reciting affirmations or visualizing your goals can help to calm your mind and allow positive thoughts to take hold.

By using affirmations and positive thinking regularly, you will be able to change your mindset and attract wealth and abundance into your life. These techniques can help you to focus your mind on what you want, to create a positive and productive mindset that will help you to achieve your financial goals.

Journaling for Manifestation

Journaling is a powerful tool that can help you to manifest wealth and abundance in your life. It allows you to track your progress, explore your thoughts and feelings, and gain clarity on your financial goals.

Here are some ways to use journaling to manifest wealth and abundance:

1. Goal Setting: Use journaling to set clear and specific financial goals. Write down the details of your goals, including the amount of money you want to earn, the assets you want to

acquire, and the lifestyle you want to create.

2. Gratitude Journaling: Use journaling to express gratitude for the good things in your life, and to focus on what you have rather than what you lack. This will help you to shift your focus from lack and scarcity to abundance and prosperity.

3. Mindset Exploration: Use journaling to explore your thoughts and beliefs about money and wealth. Identify any limiting beliefs and explore how they may be holding you back from manifesting wealth and abundance.

4. Progress Tracking: Use journaling to track your progress towards your financial goals. Write down the actions you take and the results you achieve. This will help you to stay motivated and on track towards your financial goals.

5. Reflection and Insight: Use journaling as a tool for reflection and insight. Take time to reflect on your thoughts and feelings, and to gain a deeper understanding of yourself and your relationship with money and wealth.

Journaling is a powerful tool that can help you to manifest wealth and abundance in your life. By using journaling regularly, you will be able to gain clarity on your financial goals, explore your thoughts and feelings, and track your progress towards manifesting wealth and abundance.

Law of Attraction and the Power of the Universe

The Law of Attraction is a powerful principle that states that like attracts like. It is the idea that we can manifest our desires by aligning our thoughts, feelings, and actions with them. When it comes to manifesting wealth and abundance, the Law of Attraction can be a powerful tool.

Here are some ways to use the Law of Attraction and the power of the universe to manifest wealth and abundance:

1. Align Your Thoughts and Actions: The Law of Attraction states that we attract what we think about, so it is important to align your thoughts and actions with your financial goals. Focus on what you want, not what you don't want.

2. Believe in the Power of the Universe: The power of the universe is immense and it can help you to manifest your desires. Believe in the power of the universe to bring you abundance and prosperity.

3. Use Affirmations and Visualization: The Law of Attraction states that we attract what we think about, so it is important to align your thoughts with your financial goals. Use affirmations and visualization to focus your

thoughts on what you want to
manifest.

4. Take Action: The Law of Attraction is
    not a magic wand, it requires action
    to manifest your desires. Take action
    towards your financial goals and align
    your actions with your thoughts and
    feelings.

5. Let Go of Control: Trust in the power
    of the universe to bring you
    abundance and prosperity. Let go of
    the need to control the outcome and
    allow the universe to work its magic.

By utilizing the Law of Attraction, you can
manifest wealth and abundance into your life.
Align your thoughts, beliefs, and actions with
your financial goals, trust in the power of the
universe and take action towards your goals. It
may not happen overnight, but with
consistency and patience, you can manifest
abundance in your life.

Case Studies and Success Stories

In this chapter, we will explore real-life examples of individuals who have successfully used the techniques outlined in this book to manifest wealth and abundance in their lives. These case studies and success stories will provide inspiration and guidance on how to apply the principles of manifestation to your own life.

1. "From Struggling to Success: How Anthony Used Affirmations and Visualization to Build a Million-Dollar Business" - Anthony was a struggling entrepreneur who felt stuck in his business. By using affirmations and visualization techniques, he was able to shift his mindset and attract new opportunities, ultimately leading to the success of his business.

2. "From Debt to Abundance: How Sarah Used the Law of Attraction to Pay off $50,000 in Debt" - Sarah was overwhelmed with debt and felt stuck in her financial situation. By using the Law of Attraction and shifting her beliefs about money, she was able to pay off $50,000 in debt and attract abundance into her life.

3. "From Minimum Wage to Six Figures: How Michael Used Journaling to Manifest a High-Paying Career" - Michael was stuck in a low-paying job and felt unfulfilled. By

using journaling to set clear financial goals and track his progress, he was able to manifest a high-paying career and achieve financial success.

4. "From Negative to Positive: How Rachel Used Gratitude Journaling to Shift Her Mindset and Attract Abundance" - Rachel was stuck in a negative mindset and felt like she was constantly lacking. By using gratitude journaling, she was able to shift her focus to the good things in her life and attract abundance into her life.

These case studies and success stories demonstrate that by applying the principles of manifestation, anyone can manifest wealth and abundance in their life. They provide inspiration and guidance on how to apply the techniques outlined in this book to your own life and achieve financial success.

Real-life examples of Wealth Manifestation

From Struggling to Success: How Anthony Used Affirmations and Visualization to Build a Million-Dollar Business

Anthony was a struggling entrepreneur who felt stuck in his business. Despite his hard work and dedication, he was unable to make a profit, and his business was going under. Frustrated and feeling hopeless, Anthony stumbled upon the concept of affirmations and visualization techniques for manifestation.

Anthony began to use affirmations and visualization techniques daily. He would visualize himself running a successful business, and he would recite positive affirmations to himself such as "I am a successful entrepreneur" and "My business is thriving." He also wrote down his goals and all the things he envisioned for his business and kept looking at them every day.

As Anthony continued to use these techniques, he began to notice a shift in his mindset. He started to believe in himself and his abilities to build a successful business. He started to see opportunities where he had previously seen only obstacles. He began to take action towards his financial goals and started to put more effort into his business.

Anthony's business started to pick up, and he began to see an increase in profits. His visualization and positive affirmations had helped him to focus on his goals, and his actions had begun to align with his thoughts. He attracted new clients and partnerships and started to expand his business.

Within a year, Anthony's business had grown from a struggling startup to a million-dollar business. He had successfully used affirmations and visualization techniques to shift his mindset and attract abundance into his life. Anthony's story is a testament to the power of manifestation, and how the right mindset and techniques can lead to success.

From Debt to Abundance: How Sarah Used the Law of Attraction to Pay off $50,000 in Debt

Sarah was overwhelmed with debt and felt stuck in her financial situation. She had accumulated $50,000 in credit card debt and student loans, and she couldn't see a way out. She felt like she was constantly struggling to make ends meet and was unable to save any money.

One day, Sarah came across the concept of the Law of Attraction, and she began to research how she could use it to improve her financial situation. She learned that the Law of Attraction is the belief that by focusing on positive or negative thoughts, one can bring about positive or negative results.

Sarah began to focus on positive thoughts and beliefs about money. She started to recite affirmations such as "I am debt-free" and "I am attracting abundance into my life." She also began to visualize herself as debt-free and living a financially comfortable life.

As Sarah continued to focus on these positive thoughts and beliefs, she began to take action towards her financial goals. She started to make a budget, cut expenses, and look for ways to increase her income. She also began to pay off her debt, starting with the smallest balances first.

As Sarah continued to take action and align her thoughts and actions towards her financial goals, she began to see a shift in her financial situation. She started to attract new opportunities for extra income, and her expenses began to decrease. She also began to pay off her debt at a faster rate than she had anticipated.

Within two years, Sarah had paid off all of her $50,000 in debt and had even saved enough money to take a vacation. She had successfully used the Law of Attraction to shift her mindset and attract abundance into her life. Her story is a testament to the power of the Law of Attraction and how aligning one's thoughts and actions with their goals can lead to financial success.

From Minimum Wage to Six Figures: How Michael Used Journaling to Manifest a High-Paying Career

Michael was stuck in a low-paying job and felt unfulfilled. He had a dream of having a high-paying career in his chosen field, but he didn't know how to make it happen. One day, Michael came across the concept of journaling for manifestation and decided to give it a try.

Michael began to journal every day, setting clear financial goals and tracking his progress. He wrote down his dream job, the salary he wanted, and the steps he needed to take to achieve it. He also wrote down his accomplishments, positive affirmations, and gratitude for what he had.

As Michael continued to journal, he began to focus on his goals and take action towards them. He started to network, attend job fairs, and apply for jobs in his field. He also began to improve his skills, taking classes and learning new things.

As Michael continued to take action and focus on his goals, he began to see a shift in his career. He was offered a high-paying job in his field, and he accepted it. Michael was able to manifest a high-paying career that not only paid him well but also fulfilled him.

Within a year, Michael's salary had increased from minimum wage to six figures. He had successfully used journaling to manifest his dream job and achieve financial success. His story is a testament to the power of journaling and how setting clear goals and tracking progress can lead to the manifestation of one's desired outcome.

From Negative to Positive: How Rachel Used Gratitude Journaling to Shift Her Mindset and Attract Abundance

Rachel had always been a negative person, always focusing on what she didn't have and what was going wrong in her life. She was unhappy with her job, her relationships, and her financial situation. One day, Rachel came across the concept of gratitude journaling and decided to give it a try.

Rachel began to journal every day, listing things she was grateful for, no matter how small or insignificant they may seem. She wrote down things like the roof over her head, the food on her table, and the people in her life. She also wrote about her goals and what she wanted to manifest in her life.

As Rachel continued to journal, she began to shift her focus from negative to positive. She started to appreciate what she had and the good things in her life. She began to see the beauty in everyday things and started to feel more content.

As Rachel continued to focus on gratitude, she began to see a shift in her life. She began to attract abundance in all areas of her life, her job, her relationships, and her finances. She was able to manifest her dream job, improve her relationships and her financial situation.

Within a year, Rachel had transformed her life. She had gone from a negative person to a positive person, and she had attracted abundance in all areas of her life. Her story is a testament to the power of gratitude and how shifting one's focus to the positive can lead to the manifestation of one's desires.

Insights and Lessons from these stories

The case studies presented in this book show that manifestation is a powerful tool that can be used to achieve financial success. Each story highlights a specific technique or approach that the individual used to manifest their desired outcome.

The first case study, "From Struggling to Success: How Anthony Used Affirmations and Visualization to Build a Million-Dollar Business," shows the power of affirmations and visualization in manifesting wealth. Anthony's story highlights the importance of aligning one's thoughts and actions with their financial goals and the power of positive thinking in attracting success.

The second case study, "From Debt to Abundance: How Sarah Used the Law of Attraction to Pay off $50,000 in Debt," illustrates the power of the Law of Attraction in manifesting abundance. Sarah's story shows how aligning one's thoughts and actions towards a specific goal can lead to financial success.

The third case study, "From Minimum Wage to Six Figures: How Michael Used Journaling to Manifest a High-Paying Career," showcases the power of journaling in manifesting one's desired outcome. Michael's story highlights the importance of setting clear goals and tracking progress in achieving financial success.

The fourth case study, "From Negative to Positive: How Rachel Used Gratitude Journaling to Shift Her Mindset and Attract Abundance," illustrates the power of gratitude in manifesting abundance. Rachel's story shows how shifting one's focus to the positive can lead to the manifestation of one's desires.

Overall, these case studies provide valuable insights into the manifestation process and the different techniques and approaches that can be used to achieve financial success. They demonstrate that with the right mindset and approach, anyone (including you) can manifest their desired outcome and achieve financial abundance.

Conclusion

As a reader of the "Money Manifestation Book," you have been provided with valuable insights and practical tools for manifesting wealth and achieving financial success. We've highlighted the power of manifestation and the role of mindset in attracting abundance and prosperity.

Some of the key takeaways from the book include:

- The importance of understanding and shifting limiting beliefs: We emphasize the role of beliefs in manifesting wealth and how limiting beliefs can hold individuals back from achieving their financial goals. By identifying and shifting these beliefs, you can remove obstacles that prevent you from manifesting wealth.

- The power of various manifestation techniques: We discussed different techniques such as visualization, affirmations, journaling, and the Law of Attraction. By learning and applying these techniques, you can increase your ability to manifest wealth.

- The importance of setting and achieving financial goals: We provided insight into the importance of setting clear financial goals, creating a plan to achieve them, and overcoming obstacles and staying motivated on the path to financial success. By setting and achieving your financial goals, you can create a path to manifest wealth.

- Real-life examples and case studies: We provided examples and case studies of real people who have successfully manifested wealth. These stories serve as inspiration and motivation for you to manifest wealth in your own life.

Overall, the "Money Like Magic" is an extremely valuable resource that can help you manifest wealth and achieve financial success. It provides practical tools and actionable steps that you can take to manifest wealth in your own life.

Final thoughts and next steps

As you come to the end of the "Money Like Magic," it's important to reflect on the powerful insights and practical tools you've been presented with. The book has highlighted the power of manifestation and the role of mindset in attracting abundance and prosperity.

It is now up to you to take the knowledge and apply it in your life. Remember that manifesting wealth is not a one-time event but a continuous process that requires consistent effort and commitment.

Here are some next steps to consider:
- Review the key takeaways and techniques discussed in the book and choose one or two that resonate with

you. Start incorporating them into your daily life and see how they work for you.

- Set clear financial goals and create a plan to achieve them. Remember to stay motivated and to not get discouraged by obstacles that may arise.

- Reflect on your limiting beliefs and work on shifting them. Remember that limiting beliefs can hold you back from achieving your financial goals.

- Use the real-life examples and case studies provided in the book as motivation and inspiration for your own journey towards manifesting wealth.

Remember that manifesting wealth is possible for anyone who is willing to put in the effort and commit to the process. By following the insights and tools provided in the "Money Like Magic," you can tap into the power of manifestation and create a path towards a financially abundant future.

Additional Resources

The "Money Like Magic" provides valuable insights and practical tools for manifesting wealth and achieving financial success, but it is not the only resource available. Here are some additional resources that can help you continue your journey towards manifesting wealth:

1. Books: There are many books available on the topic of manifestation and wealth creation, such as "Think and Grow Rich" by

Napoleon Hill, "The Secret" by Rhonda Byrne, and "You Are a Badass at Making Money" by Jen Sincero. These books provide additional insights and strategies for manifesting wealth.

2. Podcasts: Podcasts like "The School of Greatness" and "The Wealthy Mindset" feature interviews with successful entrepreneurs and financial experts who share their insights and strategies for creating wealth.

3. Online Courses: There are various online courses available that focus on manifestation and wealth creation. These can be a great way to dive deeper into the topics covered in the book, and provide more structured guidance and support.

4. Personal Development Programs: Some personal development programs provide training on manifestation and wealth creation. These programs often include workshops, coaching, and mentoring, which can be an effective way to stay motivated and on track with your goals.

5. Support Groups: Joining a support group of people who are also working on manifesting wealth can be a great way to stay motivated and get support when you need it. They can also be a great place to share your progress and learn from others.

Remember that manifesting wealth is a lifelong journey, and it's important to continue learning and growing along the way. These additional resources can help you stay motivated and on track as you work towards manifesting wealth in your own life.

Appendices - Exercises and worksheets to facilitate implementation

The exercises and worksheets provided in the appendices are designed to help you implement the concepts and techniques presented in "Money Like Magic." These exercises and worksheets are designed to be used in conjunction with the book and will help you to put the information into practice.

1. Limiting Beliefs Worksheet: This worksheet is designed to help you identify your limiting beliefs about money and wealth. It will also help you to shift these limiting beliefs and replace them with empowering ones.

2. Financial Goals Worksheet: This worksheet is designed to help you define your financial vision and set specific, measurable goals. It will also help you create a plan to achieve these goals.

3. Visualization Scripts: A collection of scripts that you can use to guide your visualization exercises. These scripts will help you focus your visualization on your financial goals and help you to create a powerful image in your mind of achieving them.

4. Affirmations and Positive Thinking Worksheet: This worksheet is designed to help you create affirmations that align with your financial goals and to establish a

positive mindset towards money and wealth.

5. Gratitude Journaling Worksheet: This worksheet is designed to help you cultivate an attitude of gratitude towards money and wealth. It will also help you to shift your mindset from scarcity to abundance.

6. The Law of Attraction Worksheet: This worksheet is designed to help you understand the law of attraction and how to apply it to manifest wealth.

By working through these exercises and worksheets, you will be better equipped to put the concepts and techniques presented in the "Money Like Magic" into practice and to achieve your financial goals.

Limiting Beliefs Worksheet

1.   What are some of your current beliefs about money and wealth?

____

____

____

____

2.   How have these beliefs affected your relationship with money and wealth in the past?

____

____

____

3.   What are some specific examples of situations in which these beliefs have held you back from achieving your financial goals?

____

____

4.   Are there any specific events or experiences from your past that may have contributed to these beliefs?

____

____

____

____

5.   Are there any patterns or themes that seem to be underlying these limiting beliefs?

____

____

____

____

6.   What are some positive and empowering beliefs about money and wealth that you would like to adopt in place of your limiting beliefs?

____

____

____

____

7.   How would you feel if you were able to fully adopt these positive and
empowering beliefs about money and wealth?

____

____

____

____

8.   Are there any specific action steps that you can take to help you shift your limiting beliefs and adopt these empowering beliefs?

____

____

____

____

9.   How will you remind yourself of these new empowering beliefs and hold yourself accountable to them?

____

____

____

____

10. How will these new beliefs serve you in the pursuit of your financial goals?

____

____

____

____

By working through this worksheet, you will be better equipped to identify your limiting beliefs about money and wealth and replace them with empowering beliefs that will help you to achieve your financial goals. Remember to focus on the positive and empowering beliefs that you want to adopt and take action to shift your limiting beliefs.

Financial Goals Worksheet

1.   What is your financial vision? Be specific and describe it in detail.

---

2.   What are your short-term financial goals? (less than 1 year)
   Example: Saving $10,000 for an emergency fund

---

3.   What are your medium-term financial goals? (1-5 years)
   Example: Paying off credit card debt

____

____

4. What are your long-term financial
goals? (more than 5 years)
   Example: Retiring with $1,000,000 in savings

____

____

____

____

5. How will achieving these goals impact
your life?

____

____

____

____

6. What steps can you take to achieve these
goals?
   *Example: Increase income, reduce expenses,
and invest.*

____

7.   What are the potential obstacles that
may prevent you from achieving these goals?

8.   How can you overcome these obstacles?
*Example: Create a budget, negotiate for a raise,
or look for a better-paying job.*

9.   What resources do you need to achieve
these goals?
*Example: Financial planning software,
financial advisor, or budgeting apps*

____

____

____

____

10. What are your deadlines for achieving these goals?

____

____

____

____

11. How will you hold yourself accountable for achieving these goals?
Example: Reviewing your goals regularly and tracking your progress.

____

____

____

____

By working through this worksheet, you will be better equipped to define your financial

vision and set specific, measurable goals. You
will also be able to identify the steps and
resources needed to achieve these goals, and
the potential obstacles and how to overcome
them. Make sure you set deadlines to keep
yourself motivated and review your progress
regularly to stay on track.

Visualization Scripts

Script 1: Attracting Abundance

Close your eyes and take a deep breath. Imagine yourself standing in front of a large, beautiful tree. This tree represents abundance and prosperity in all areas of your life.

See the branches of the tree reaching high into the sky, and the roots of the tree spreading deep into the earth.

As you focus on the tree, notice the leaves rustling in the wind, and the branches swaying. This tree is alive and thriving, and it represents all the abundance and prosperity that you desire.

As you gaze at the tree, notice that it is surrounded by a bright, white light. This light represents the positive energy and good luck that is flowing towards you.

As you continue to focus on the tree, feel yourself becoming one with it. You are now a part of the tree, and you are tapping into its abundance and prosperity.

As you feel this connection to the tree, see yourself achieving all of your financial goals. Imagine yourself buying your dream home, paying off all of your debts, and having more than enough money to live the life you've always wanted.

As you hold onto this vision, take one last deep breath, and when you're ready, open your eyes.

Script 2: Achieving Financial Freedom

Close your eyes and take a deep breath. Imagine yourself standing on the top of a mountain. This mountain represents financial freedom and independence.

Look around you, and see the beautiful landscape that surrounds you. The mountain represents all the hard work and effort you've put in to achieve your financial goals.

As you stand at the top of the mountain, feel the sense of accomplishment and pride that comes with achieving your goals.

Now look out into the horizon and imagine yourself living the life of your dreams. See yourself traveling to exotic places, buying the things you've always wanted, and living without worry or stress about money.

As you hold onto this vision, take one last deep breath, and when you're ready, open your eyes.

Script 3: Manifesting a High-Paying Career

Close your eyes and take a deep breath. Imagine yourself walking into a beautiful office building. This building represents your dream job.

As you walk through the building, notice how it feels. The atmosphere is professional, yet welcoming. You feel a sense of belonging and excitement.

As you approach the door of your office, take a moment to feel the energy of the space. You can feel the success, the recognition and the high pay that comes with this job.

As you step inside the office, see yourself sitting at the desk. You are the CEO, the manager, the executive or the specialist in your field. You are respected and valued.

As you look around the office, see all the things you have always wanted. The window with a view, the plant, the photos of your family, the awards and the certificates.

As you hold onto this vision, take one last deep breath, and when you're ready, open your eyes.

--

These visualization scripts are designed to help you focus your thoughts and energy on achieving your financial goals. They are a powerful tool to help you manifest the abundance and prosperity you desire. Remember to close your eyes, take deep breaths, and focus on the details of the scene you are visualizing.

Affirmations and Positive Thinking Worksheet

1. I am worthy and deserving of abundance and prosperity in all areas of my life.

2. I am capable and confident in my ability to achieve my financial goals.

3. I am surrounded by positive energy and good luck that helps me to attract wealth.

4. I am grateful for the abundance and prosperity that is already present in my life.

5. I trust in the Universe to guide me towards the perfect opportunities for financial success.

6. I am open to receiving abundance and prosperity in unexpected ways.

7. I release all limiting beliefs and negative thoughts about money and abundance.

8. I choose to focus on abundance and prosperity and let go of scarcity and lack.

9. I am willing to take action towards my financial goals and trust the process.

10. I am thankful for the abundance and prosperity that is on its way to me now.

Instructions:

- Read each affirmation out loud, with conviction and enthusiasm

- Repeat affirmations as much as you want and feel them.

- Write them down and place them where you can see them daily.

- Try to integrate them in your daily routine.

By repeating these affirmations and incorporating positive thinking into your mindset, you can shift your beliefs and attract more abundance and prosperity in your life.

Gratitude Journaling Worksheet

1. Today, I am grateful for:

____

____

____

____

2. Something that made me feel happy today:

____

____

____

____

3. Something that I accomplished today:

____

____

____

____

4. Something that I am looking forward to tomorrow:

____

____

____

____

5. A person who has helped me today:

____

____

____

____

6. A thing that I have that I am thankful for:

____

____

____

____

7. Something that I have learned today:

____

____

____

____

8. A moment of kindness or generosity I have experienced today

____

____

____

____

9. Something that I am proud of today

____

____

____

____

10. A positive affirmation that I am focusing
on today

____

____

____

____

Instructions:

•	Take a few minutes each day to reflect
and write down what you are grateful for.

•	Try to come up with new things each day
to write about.
•	Reflect on how each thing you are
grateful for has positively impacted your life.

•	Try to find the positive and good in all
aspects of your life, including difficult
situations.

•	Re-read your entries regularly and use it
as a source of inspiration and motivation.

Gratitude journaling is a powerful tool to
shift your mindset, focus on the positive
aspects of your life and attract more abundance
and prosperity.

The Law of Attraction Worksheet

1. My current financial situation:

---

2. My desired financial situation:

---

3. Specific financial goals that I want to achieve:

4.　The actions I am willing to take to
achieve my goals:

____

____

____

____

5.　Obstacles that I anticipate facing:

____

____

____

____

6.　Ways I can overcome these obstacles:

____

____

____

____

7.   Positive affirmations that align with my financial goals:

____

____

____

____

8.   Visualizations that align with my financial goals:

____

____

____

____

9.   Gratitude statements for what I already have in my life:

____

____

____

____

10. Things I can do to stay motivated and focused on my goals:

____

____

____

____

Instructions:

- Use this worksheet to clarify your financial goals and desired outcome.

- Take time to visualize and feel as if you have already achieved your goals.

- Incorporate positive affirmations, visualization and gratitude into your daily routine.

- Be specific in your goals and think about what actions you will take to achieve them.

- Prepare for obstacles and think about ways to overcome them.

- Use this worksheet as a reminder of your goals and to help stay focused and motivated.

By aligning your thoughts and actions with the Law of Attraction, you can manifest the abundance and prosperity you desire in your life.

Glossary of Key Terms

- **Abundance:** A state of having more than enough of something, often used to refer to wealth, resources, or opportunities.

- **Affirmations:** Positive statements or declarations used to reprogram the mind and reinforce desired beliefs and behaviors.

- **Gratitude:** The practice of being thankful and showing appreciation for what one has.

- **Law of Attraction:** The belief that like attracts like, and that by focusing on positive or negative thoughts, one can bring about positive or negative results.

- **Limiting beliefs:** False or negative beliefs about oneself or the world that hold one back from achieving their goals.

- **Manifestation:** The process of bringing something into reality through focused thoughts and actions.

- **Mindset:** A person's attitude, thoughts, and beliefs that shape their perception of the world and themselves.

- **Obstacles:** Anything that gets in the way of achieving a goal or desired outcome.

- **Positive thinking:** The practice of focusing on the positive aspects of life, rather than the negative.

- **Visualization:** The practice of creating mental images of a desired outcome to manifest it into reality.

These key terms are commonly used in the context of manifestation and the Law of Attraction and understanding them is crucial to understanding the techniques and principles outlined in the Book.

About The Author

Louis 'Lou' Sefer is a dedicated occult, spiritual, and metaphysical student. He has studied the teachings of different esoteric, magickal, and mystical schools and practices over the years, as well as hundreds of books on the subjects.

Obsessed with gathering, researching, and assimilation of ancient knowledge in search of the truth. He has an honorary Doctor of Divinity from one institution. He is also an ordained minister. He prefers to remain anonymous.

Author of the Best Seller 'Sacred Secrets of Esoteric Christianity' and 'Mysteries of the Soul' both available for sale on Amazon.

Additional Readings and References

1. "The Secret" by Rhonda Byrne: This bestselling book provides an introduction to the Law of Attraction and how to use it to manifest wealth and abundance in one's life.

2. "Think and Grow Rich" by Napoleon Hill: Written in the 1930s, this classic book explores the power of positive thinking and how to manifest wealth and success through visualization and goal setting.

3. "The Power of Intention" by Dr. Wayne Dyer: This book explores the concept of manifesting one's desires through the power of intention, and provides practical exercises and techniques for doing so.

4. "The Science of Getting Rich" by Wallace D. Wattles: This book, written in 1910, is considered one of the first books on the Law of Attraction and provides a detailed guide on how to manifest wealth and abundance in one's life.

5. "You Are a Badass at Making Money" by Jen Sincero: This New York Times Bestseller is a practical and funny guide on how to overcome limiting beliefs around money and to manifest wealth and success.

6. "The Wealthy Mindset: How to
    Develop a Winning Mindset and
    Achieve Financial Freedom" by Steve
    Seabold: This book explores the
    connection between mindset and
    wealth and provides practical
    strategies to develop a wealthy
    mindset and achieve financial
    freedom.

These books and authors are considered
experts in the field of manifestation, wealth
and success, and provide valuable insights,
strategies and inspiration that can be helpful in
the journey of manifesting wealth and
abundance in your life.